BENJAMIN
FRANKLIN
SCIENTIST AND STATESMAN

BENJAMIN
FRANKLIN
SCIENTIST AND STATESMAN

by Brenda Haugen
and Andrew Santella

Content Adviser: Richard J. Bell,
History Department, Harvard University

Reading Adviser: Rosemary G. Palmer, Ph.D.,
Department of Literacy, College of Education,
Boise State University

COMPASS POINT BOOKS ✦ MINNEAPOLIS, MINNESOTA

JB Franklin
Haugen

Compass Point Books
3109 West 50th Street, #115
Minneapolis, MN 55410

Visit Compass Point Books on the Internet at *www.compasspointbooks.com*
or e-mail your request to *custserv@compasspointbooks.com*

Editor: Jennifer VanVoorst
Lead Designer: Jaime Martens
Photo Researcher: Svetlana Zhurkina
Page Production: Heather Griffin
Cartographer: XNR Productions, Inc.
Educational Consultant: Diane Smolinski

Managing Editor: Catherine Neitge
Art Director: Keith Griffin
Production Director: Keith McCormick
Creative Director: Terri Foley

To Todd McCord. Thank you for all your support and encouragement.
I love you! BLH

Library of Congress Cataloging-in-Publication Data
Haugen, Brenda.
  Benjamin Franklin : scientist and statesman / by Brenda Haugen and
Andrew Santella.
       p. cm. — (Signature lives)
  Includes bibliographical references and index.
  ISBN 0-7565-0826-6 (hardcover)
  1. Franklin, Benjamin, 1706-1790—Juvenile literature. 2. Statesmen—
United States—Biography—Juvenile literature. 3. Scientists—United
States—Biography—Juvenile literature. 4. Inventors—United States—
Biography—Juvenile literature. 5. Printers—United States—Biography—
Juvenile literature. I. Santella, Andrew. II. Title. III. Series.
E302.6.F8H37 2005
973.3'092—dc22   2004023194

REVOLUTIONARY WAR ERA

The American Revolution created heroes—and traitors—
who shaped the birth of a new nation: the United States
of America. "Taxation without representation" was a serious
problem for the American colonies during the late 1700s.
Great Britain imposed harsh taxes and didn't give the
colonists a voice in their own government. The colonists
rebelled and declared their independence from Britain—
the war was on.

Table of Contents

1 BENJAMIN FRANKLIN'S RETURN

ఇఆఅ

The news quickly spread through the busy streets of Philadelphia. Benjamin Franklin was coming home. It was 1775, and Philadelphia's favorite son had been in England for nearly 18 years. Now he was returning home at a time when he was badly needed. A huge crowd gathered to welcome their city's hero. Franklin's daughter, Sarah Bache, and her family led the way. Franklin had never seen Sarah's youngest son, also named Benjamin, who was now about 6 years old. Franklin had missed so much while he was away.

Arriving in Philadelphia on May 5, 1775, Franklin found his city buzzing with talk of war and rebellion. For years, American colonists had been complaining that Great Britain's government was not treating

In his lifetime, Benjamin Franklin was successful in many fields, including printing, science, and politics.

In 1775, British troops clashed with American volunteer soldiers called Minutemen in Lexington, Massachusetts.

them fairly. Finally, the colonists' angry protests turned into violent conflict. In April, British soldiers and American militia clashed in bloody battles in Massachusetts. In Philadelphia and throughout the 13 colonies, people prepared for war.

Franklin had hoped the British and the American colonists could work out their differences peacefully. He had many close friends in Britain. To him, the city of London felt almost as much like home as Philadelphia. Even so, now that war had arrived, Franklin embraced the American cause.

The day after Franklin returned to Philadelphia, he was elected to represent Pennsylvania in the Second Continental Congress. Later he negotiated France's help in the war against Great Britain. Franklin's work played an important part in securing American independence.

Franklin was 69 years old when he returned home to Philadelphia. He had already lived a full life. He had built a successful printing business, making himself wealthy in the process. His inventions and experiments with electricity had won him fame and respect. He could have retired and rested, secure in his fame. He could have spent more time with his family, which was something he had sacrificed in order to serve his fellow colonists. Instead, Franklin jumped into the fight for freedom. He still had important work to do.

Because of his work in the diverse fields of science, literature, and politics, and his expertise in trades such as printing and candle-making, Benjamin Franklin is often called America's Renaissance Man. This title refers to a time period in Europe—the 14th–16th centuries—when artists such as Leonardo da Vinci were skilled in many different areas.

2 BOSTON BOYHOOD

❧❦❧

Long before he began working for American independence, the young Benjamin Franklin displayed an independent streak of his own. He spent much of his childhood struggling against the wishes of his father.

Benjamin Franklin was born in Boston, Massachusetts, on a cold, blustery Sunday—January 17, 1706. Though they didn't have much money, the Franklin family was rich with love. Ben's father, Josiah Franklin, had come to Boston from England in 1683. He made soap and candles for a living. Ben's mother, Abiah Folger, married Josiah after the death of Josiah's first wife. With wives from two marriages, Josiah fathered a total of 17 children. Ben, the youngest son, was the 15th child.

When Benjamin Franklin was a boy, Boston was a busy shipping port and the largest city in North America.

Being one of the youngest children, Ben quickly learned to use his wits rather than force to get his way. His older siblings not only outweighed him, they outnumbered him.

They were also quick to point out any mistake Ben might make. One lesson they taught him involved the value of money and how wasting it makes a person look foolish. When Ben was 7, some friends gave him money as a gift. Years later, Ben remembered:

> *I went directly to a shop where they sold toys for children, and being charmed with the sound of a whistle that I met by the way, in the hands of another boy, I voluntarily offered and gave all my money for it. When I came home, whistling all over the house, much pleased with my whistle, but disturbing all the family, my brothers, sisters and cousins, understanding the bargain I had made, told me I had given four times as much for it as it was worth, put me in mind of what good things I might have bought with the rest of the money, and laughed at me so much for my folly that I cried with vexation; and the reflection gave me more chagrin than the whistle gave me pleasure. ... As I came into the world, and observed the actions of men, I thought I met many who gave too much for the whistle.*

Benjamin Franklin was born in this home on Milk Street in Boston, Massachusetts.

The Franklin home buzzed with activity. Josiah often invited educated people to share his family's simple evening meals. Josiah wanted his children to benefit from hearing intelligent conversation. Music often filled the Franklin household, too. With his beautiful voice, Josiah sang hymns in the evening while playing the violin. Ben inherited Josiah's love of music and learned to play the violin, harp, guitar, and other instruments.

Ben also loved the sea. He grew up just a short walk away from Boston Harbor. Boston was then the busiest seaport in North America, with ships

Ben was named after his uncle Benjamin, Josiah's favorite brother. For many years, Uncle Benjamin continued to live in England. When Ben was old enough to read and write, he borrowed Josiah's ink-well and quill pen and wrote many long letters to Uncle Benjamin. Ben always enjoyed writing to adults.

from around the world making regular stops there.

Ben spent many of his early days playing along the Boston waterfront. He learned to swim and handle small boats when he was still very young. He made a pair of wooden flippers and hand paddles to help himself swim better. One day, he used a kite to catch the wind and pull himself across a pond as he floated in the water.

Ben was a leader among his friends, and he often came up with ideas for projects that involved them, too. Sometimes his ideas got them all into trouble, though. Once, the boys got tired of standing on the boggy soil at their favorite fishing pond. When Ben spied a pile of rocks set aside to build the foundation of a house, he got an idea. He told his friends to meet him back at the pond that evening.

When evening came, the boys arrived as promised. Ben and his friends collected the pile of rocks and made a dock out of them. Now they could fish in comfort without getting wet.

In the morning, the house builders saw what had happened to their rocks and were hopping mad. When they discovered the identities of the boys, the builders went to talk to the boys' parents.

Josiah confronted Ben about what he had done, but Ben argued that his project was truly useful, not just an act of theft. "Nothing is useful that is not honest," Josiah said. Ben knew Josiah was right, and it was a lesson about honesty Ben would never forget.

Josiah was known for being honest and fair. Leaders in the community often asked his opinion on important issues. He also helped settle private disputes by serving as an arbitrator when asked. With 17 children, Josiah likely had to use these same skills to settle arguments at home, too.

While Josiah didn't always side with him in arguments, Ben was Josiah's favorite child. Josiah realized Ben was fascinated by the big ships in the harbor and dreamed of sailing away from Boston to live on the high seas, as one of his older brothers had done. Josiah, however, had other ideas for Ben.

When Ben was just 8 years old, Josiah decided that Ben would become a minister. Josiah enrolled his son in the local grammar school, where Ben quickly went to the top of his class. Josiah soon realized, though, that he couldn't afford to send Ben to college to become a minister. He dropped his plans for educating Ben for the ministry and sent him to a school where he'd learn more about writing and math. ❧

3 THE YOUNG APPRENTICE

ec×no

When Ben was 10, Josiah decided Ben should learn a useful trade. After just two years of formal education, Ben quit school and went off to work. Josiah decided Ben would serve as an apprentice in his candle-making shop. Serving as an apprentice was a common path for boys like Ben. They worked for master tradesmen for several years, and in the process they learned the skills that would help them make a living for the rest of their lives. Josiah hoped Ben would follow in his footsteps and one day take over the family business.

Ben filled candle molds, cut candlewicks, ran errands for his father, and watched the shop when needed. But Ben hated making candles. He found the work boring, and the long hours seemed endless

Young Ben Franklin learned the craft of printing by working as an apprentice in his brother James's print shop.

As a boy, Ben Franklin poured fat into molds in his father's candle shop.

to him. Worse yet, the job literally stunk. Candles were made from the fat of cows and sheep, and the smell of boiling animal fat filled the shop. Sometimes Josiah gave Ben some coins for working in the shop. Almost immediately, Ben would run off to buy reading materials. He read magazines, books, newspapers—whatever he could find. Staying up late at night, Ben read by candlelight. He shared a room with one of his older brothers, but his brother always fell asleep right away and wasn't bothered by the light.

Ben's family was so poor, he couldn't ask for new candles to read by. Instead, he collected stubs of old candles that neighbors threw out. He used these stubs to read by after the sun went down. The stubs burned out quickly, but Ben used one to light the next as he continued to read. When Ben's parents discovered he was reading until after midnight, they told him to make sure he was getting enough sleep, but they didn't discourage him from reading. His mother even tried to find bigger candles to give him whenever she could spare them.

While Ben enjoyed having the money to buy books, Josiah knew Ben was unhappy working at the candle shop. Josiah also was afraid that Ben would run off to sea rather than continue working at something he hated. So, Josiah came up with another plan.

This time, he decided, Ben would go to work for his half brother James. Ten years older than Ben, James Franklin already owned a successful printing business. Being a printer sounded better to Ben than being a candle maker. At least printers worked with the written word. At the age of 12, Ben became a printer's apprentice.

James and Ben drew up and

One of Ben's older brothers, Josiah, had run off to be a sailor, which strengthened his father's will to find Ben a trade that would keep him on land. Ben's brother would be lost at sea and never heard from again.

signed a contract. James would provide Ben with meals, clothes, and a place to live. In return, Ben would work for James for nine years. By then, Ben would turn 21 and be ready to go out on his own.

At first, Ben's duties were limited to sweeping, cleaning up the shop, and running errands. Soon he began to learn more about the printer's trade.

The printing process was slow and involved many steps. Each page of text needed to be inked by hand.

Printers like James produced everything from posters and newspapers to books using a process that would seem very slow and difficult today. To produce a line of text, Ben lined up small metal let-

ters in neat rows. When he had lined up enough letters to make a page of text, he placed the rows of letters in a wooden frame to hold them in place. Then he covered the letters in ink. Finally, he put a sheet of paper over the letters and pressed the paper into the ink. When he pulled the paper away, it was covered in lines of inky text.

> *Ben didn't mind borrowing books from others, but he liked owning books, too. While working for James, Ben lived part of the time as a vegetarian. By not eating meat, Ben was able to save about half his weekly allowance, which he then used to buy more books.*

The process was slow, and printers had to put in long hours. It was hard work, too. Ben had to lift heavy sets of metal letters and use his muscle power to operate the printing press.

His job wasn't the only thing keeping Ben busy. Ben was determined to educate himself. His new job gave him access to a variety of books and newspapers, and Ben was eager to read them all. "Often I sat up in my room reading the greatest part of the night," he later remembered.

In 1721, James began publishing a newspaper called the *New England Courant*. Ben helped him print and deliver the papers, but he wanted to do more.

Some of James's friends wrote articles for the *Courant*. When they visited, Ben listened in on their conversations and dreamed of writing for the paper himself.

The first issue of the New England Courant came out on August 7, 1721. The Courant was the first American newspaper not owned and edited by a post- , master. In those days, postmasters could mail newspapers for free. They also could stop other newspapers from being delivered, if they so chose. Ben helped deliver his brother's newspaper to make sure it reached its subscribers.

To improve his writing skills, Ben tried to copy the best writers of the time. He even wrote several poems about current events, which his brother had printed and sold on the street.

Ben knew, however, that his older brother thought he wasn't old enough or educated enough to write for the *Courant*. So Ben secretly left his articles under the door of the print shop for James to find.

The articles were signed by a woman named Silence Dogood, but in fact Silence Dogood was really Ben Franklin. James liked Silence's articles so much that he printed them in the paper. James's friends started discussing Silence's work when they visited the print shop.

Encouraged, Ben continued to submit more and more articles. Neither James nor any of the paper's readers knew who Silence Dogood really was. When Ben finally told his brother he had been writing the articles, James was furious that his younger brother had tricked him. Ben later wrote that the hot-tempered James beat him for deceiving him.

As Ben grew older, he assumed more and more

responsibility in the shop. In June 1722, James published a fake letter to the editor in the *Courant* that he had written himself. He criticized town leaders for not seriously pursuing pirates who were causing trouble that season along the New England coast. James was no stranger to writing articles in his newspaper that made city officials angry, but when he was discovered to be the author of the letter, the Massachusetts General Court took action this time and threw him in jail. While James sat in jail for a month, Ben ran the newspaper for him.

Ben Franklin sold copies of his poem, "The Lighthouse Tragedy," on the street.

Once out of jail, James didn't stay out of trouble for long. By early 1723, he again was writing articles that made town leaders angry. To stop him, the General Court forbid James to print his newspaper unless town officials reviewed it before it was sold. Outraged, James came up with a plan. The order applied only to him, not to Ben. Why not publish the *Courant* under Ben's name?

Both James and Ben knew that no one would ever believe James would let an apprentice indentured to him run the *Courant*. But if Ben were a free man, no one could prove he wasn't running the newspaper. So, James agreed to sign Ben's original indenture, saying he was released from the contract. This would prove to the sheriff and other town officials that Ben was a free man. He really wasn't, though. James made Ben sign a second, secret agreement saying he remained indentured to James until he turned 21. Publicly Ben was free, but secretly he was not.

Ben agreed to the plan, though. This was his big chance to have more influence over what was printed in the *Courant*. In time, the newspaper started to take on more of Ben's wit and personality.

Ben loved the work, but hated working with James. The brothers continued to argue, and Ben sometimes suffered more beatings at his brother's hands. Eventually, Ben had enough.

Ben and his brother James did not get along well.

The experience Ben gained at James's shop taught Ben he was ready to run his own business. However, he still owed James several more years of service as an apprentice. If Ben wanted his independence, he had only one choice. He would have to run away. 🍂

27 ⌒⌒

Chapter
4 LIFE ON HIS OWN

❧❦❧

Ben Franklin was 17 years old when he decided to leave Boston. It was no easy decision. He still owed James nearly four more years of service as an apprentice. Running away from Boston meant breaking the law.

But Franklin was determined to go out on his own. He knew James would never say anything about the secret indenture agreement. If he did, James would have to admit he, not his brother, was really the publisher of the *Courant* and risk going to jail himself.

Though James wouldn't say anything about the secret agreement, Franklin knew James would tell other printers in Boston not to hire him. He would have to leave town to find another job.

When Benjamin Franklin arrived in Philadelphia, he was dirty, rumpled, and jobless.

Franklin made his decision. Having little money, he sold his precious books. He then traveled more than 200 miles (320 kilometers) to New York City to find a job in a print shop. After three days, Franklin arrived in town only to discover there was no work to be found. New York printer William Bradford said he had all the help he needed at his print shop, but his son Andrew was looking for someone to help in his shop in Philadelphia, Pennsylvania.

With no other prospects, Franklin traveled the 100 miles to Philadelphia. The journey proved extremely difficult. The first part of the trip, he sailed in a small, old boat with the boat owner and one other passenger. Hit by a violent windstorm, the boat's old sails ripped like thin sheets of paper. As the boat rocked violently back and forth, the other passenger fell overboard. Franklin reacted quickly. He grabbed the man and pulled him back into the boat.

The group remained in danger, though, as winds continued to pummel the small vessel. As the wind dragged the boat closer and closer to the shore of Long Island and its rocky beach, the men threw out the anchor to keep the boat from crashing into the shore. They knew the rickety vessel would be destroyed if it hit the rough beach.

As the storm wailed on, Franklin and the two other men huddled together as protection against the cold, pounding waves and rain. Though the night seemed endless, morning eventually came, and the storm quieted. They had made it safely through the storm!

Franklin suffered on the boat for 30 hours without sleep, food, or water. When he reached New Jersey, he still had a 50-mile (80-kilometer) walk before reaching Philadelphia. On top of it all, he became ill with a high fever, so he found a place to stay. He drank lots of water and got a good night's sleep. The next morning he awoke refreshed, ready to start his walk to Philadelphia despite the continuing rain.

On October 6, 1723, after four days of travel, Franklin arrived in Philadelphia. He later admitted that he must have made "a most awkward, ridiculous appearance" on his first day. "I was dirty from my journey; my pockets were stuffed out with shirts and stockings, and I knew no soul nor where to look for lodging," Franklin wrote.

Having gone without bathing for days, Franklin walked down Market Street in his dirty clothes and looked for a place to stay. As he walked, he saw a boy with a loaf of bread. The boy gave him directions to the bakery. Franklin had very little money, and he asked the baker what he could get for three cents. The baker sold him three big, fluffy rolls. "I was surprised at the quantity, but took it, and, having no room in my pockets, walked off with a roll under each arm and eating the other," Franklin remembered later.

He also remembered a pretty girl who giggled at him as he walked past her on the street. Little did he know, she would later play an important part in his life.

Franklin may have appeared awkward and ridiculous on his first day in Philadelphia, but he soon started a new life there. Though Andrew Bradford already had hired an assistant, he suggested Franklin talk to Samuel Keimer. New to Philadelphia, Keimer was starting another print shop in town.

Keimer offered Franklin a job and found a place for him to live. He would stay with the Read family, friends of Keimer. Eighteen-year-old Deborah Read barely recognized Franklin once he was all cleaned up. She was the girl who giggled at his appearance on his first day in Philadelphia.

Eventually, Deborah and Ben fell in love. Franklin hoped to set up his own business and then get married. His opportunity came in 1724.

William Keith, the governor of Pennsylvania, was shown a letter Franklin had written to his brother-in-law. Keith was impressed with the young man. He visited Franklin at Keimer's shop and offered to set Franklin up with his own print shop. The governor suggested Franklin sail to England to pick out the equipment he would need to get his business started. Keith promised to send letters of credit along with Franklin

Governor Keith encouraged Franklin to go to England to get supplies for his new print shop.

so he could buy whatever he desired. Franklin jumped at the chance.

In Franklin's time, the trip from North America to England required a long and sometimes dangerous ocean crossing. Travelers could spend six weeks or longer on a cramped, uncomfortable ship before they reached their destination.

Ben Franklin hoped to marry Deborah Read after his return from England.

Franklin wanted to marry Deborah, but at only 18 years old, he felt they both were very young. Furthermore, Franklin felt he was still too poor to

take a wife. He also faced a long voyage, as well as time in England buying supplies. Franklin talked to Deborah's mother. He agreed with her that it would be best to wait to marry Deborah until he returned from England and was set up in his printing business.

Franklin left for England on the ship *London Hope* on November 2, 1724. The trip took nearly two months. Franklin passed the time by talking with other passengers and playing checkers and cards.

The ship pitched and rolled through storms on its long journey across the Atlantic Ocean. *London Hope* was strong, though, and held together. It finally arrived in London, England, on December 24.

Eager to get his equipment and be on his way back home, Franklin opened the letters of credit from Governor Keith. To his horror, Franklin discovered the bag Keith gave him was full of papers, but none were letters of credit. Thomas Denham, a Philadelphia merchant Franklin met on the trip to England, said he wasn't surprised. Keith had no money, Denham said. "He wished to please everybody, and having little to give, he gave expectations," Denham told Franklin.

Three thousand miles from home, Franklin found himself with no money and no way to get back home. He immediately began searching for a job and found one in a London print shop.

Franklin quickly impressed his boss. While most

printers used both hands to carry one large set of type, Franklin could carry two—one in each hand. At 18 years old, Franklin was nearly 6 feet tall with a strong, muscular frame. He didn't waste time, and

Franklin worked on this printing press when he lived in England.

he worked longer and harder than just about anyone else in the shop.

Franklin saved all the money he could, but after nearly two years, he still hadn't earned enough for the trip back to Philadelphia. In the fall of 1726, Thomas Denham offered to pay Franklin's way back to the colonies and to give him a job as a clerk in his Philadelphia store. Franklin gladly accepted the offer, promising himself to be frugal with his money until he had paid Denham back.

"I was grown tired of London, remember'd with great pleasure the happy months I had spent in Pennsylvania, and wish'd again to see it," Franklin later wrote. He had been in London for nearly two years, and he could hardly wait to get home. 🕮

5 CITIZEN FRANKLIN OF PHILADELPHIA

Chapter

∽◌◇◌∾

Aboard the *Berkshire*, Franklin and Denham set sail for Pennsylvania on July 21, 1726. Franklin used the time on the ship to think about his life and what was important to him. He thought about the kind of person he wanted to become.

Arriving in Philadelphia on October 11, Ben discovered he couldn't just pick up his life where he had left it. Deborah had married someone else, but she was miserable. Deborah's husband had piled up a great amount of debt and then left her. There were also rumors that he had another wife.

Franklin blamed himself for Deborah's misfortunes. Had he married Deborah before he left, none of this would have happened to her. When in England, he had only bothered to write her one letter.

Benjamin Franklin founded the Philadelphia Union Fire Company and the first insurance organization in North America.

Why would she wait for him? Franklin felt terrible. He vowed to be a better person. He would treat others better than he had been treated by Keith— better than Deborah had been treated by her husband. He would be honest, frugal, and hardworking.

Franklin also vowed to serve his community, outside of his workday. To achieve this goal, he formed Junto, a club in which people could share ideas and work to improve society. This type of club was popular in Europe, but only educated men were allowed to join. Junto, Franklin decided, would be limited to 12 members who had curiosity and wanted to improve themselves, educated or not.

The club met each Friday. Members talked about history, science, travel, politics, and morality. Each week, members would raise questions on these subjects for the group to discuss. They talked about laws—whether new ones were needed or old ones were working. In addition, every three months, each member wrote an essay on something he found interesting. These, too, were discussed by the group.

Franklin kept busy with work and Junto, but a battle with pleurisy slowed him down for some time. Six months after Franklin returned from England, both he and Thomas Denham fell ill and had to close the shop. Although Franklin slowly recovered, Denham died. Denham left Franklin a small amount of money in his will. The money was enough to let Ben recover at home without worrying. Denham's shop, however, never reopened.

Franklin was out of work again, but once his health returned, he quickly found another job. Samuel Keimer offered him a position teaching his apprentices. Franklin didn't realize Keimer was just using him to get his shop running properly. When the apprentices were trained, Keimer picked a fight with Franklin and then fired him. Franklin was so angry that he left the shop without taking his possessions.

Ben Franklin displays the printing press in his shop in Philadelphia.

Hugh Meredith, one of Franklin's friends from the shop, visited him later that evening to return the items he had left behind. Meredith told Franklin he thought he'd been treated unfairly. The son of a wealthy farmer, Meredith said he thought he could come up with the money to set up a new print shop if Franklin would be his business partner. Meredith's father would supply the money to get the shop going if Franklin would teach Meredith the printing trade. Franklin readily agreed.

Business was slow when the new shop opened in 1728, but they did get a small job right away, thanks to one of Franklin's Junto friends. As word spread about what good work the shop did, more business headed their way.

Franklin also wanted to start a newspaper, but there already were two in Philadelphia. Franklin didn't believe the town of 7,000 could support three newspapers. He soon got his chance to be a newsman, though. One of the city's newspapers, the *Pennsylvania Gazette*, was printed by Franklin's old boss, Samuel Keimer. Unable to write well or spend much time collecting news, Keimer decided to sell the newspaper in order to devote more time to his print shop. Keimer was willing to sell the newspaper cheap, just to get rid of it.

In Franklin's day, news was usually collected and printed by the newspaper publishers. Publishers didn't hire reporters as they do today.

Franklin and Meredith bought the paper from Keimer. Their first issue of the *Pennsylvania Gazette* hit the streets on October 2, 1729.

Franklin wanted the newspaper to be successful. He worked hard to fill it with news people needed to know. He also used his sense of humor and printed lively stories that would make people want to pick up each issue. He made sure his stories were accurate.

JANUARY 15. 1739,40. NUMB. 579.

The Pennsylvania GAZETTE.

Containing the freshest Ad- *vices Foreign and Domestick.*

PHILADELPHIA.

On Friday last the Governor sent down to the House of Representatives the following MESSAGE, *in Answer to their* ADDRESS *of the 5th Instant.*

His Honour the Governor in Council to the Gentlemen of the Assembly.

GENTLEMEN,

YOUR dutiful Expressions of his Majesty, your Gratitude for the many Blessings you enjoy under his Government, and the just Sense you entertain of my Concern for the Safety of the Province, notwithstanding our Difference of Opinion in other Matters, render your Address very acceptable to me. I should have thought my self happy not to have been laid under a Necessity, by the Posture of Affairs in *Europe,* of pressing a Matter so disagreeable to the Religious Sentiments of many of the Inhabitants of this Province; but as I think my self indispensibly obliged by the Duty I owe to his Majesty, in Discharge of the Trust reposed in me by your honourable Proprietors, and from a disinterested Regard for the Lives and Fortunes of the People under my Government, to warn you of the impending Danger, I hope you likewise, will have patience with me, and continue to entertain the same charitable Sentiments of my Intentions.

In my Speech to you at your first Meeting, I considered you as the Representatives of the whole Body of the People, as a part of the Legislature, and as Protestants, and as such I desired you to turn your Thoughts upon the defenceless State of the Province, and to put yourselves into such a Condition, as becomes loyal Subjects to his Majesty, and Lovers of your Religion and Liberties. As it did not become me to distinguish the particular Religious Persuasion of every Member of your House, I could speak of your Religion no otherwise than in Contradistinction to the bloody Religion of *France* and *Spain*: But now, from what you yourselves have declared, I must lament the unhappy Circumstances of a Country, populous indeed, extensive in its Trade, blessed with many natural Advantages, and capable of defending itself, but from a religious Principle of its Representatives against bearing of Arms, subject to become the Prey of the first Invader, and more particularly of its powerful Neighbours, who are known to be well armed, regular in their Discipline, inured to Fatigue, and from thence capable of making long Marches, in Alliance with many Nations of *Indians,* and of a boundless Ambition.

Far be it from me to attempt the least Invasion on your Charter, or your Laws for Liberty of Conscience, or to engage any Assembly in Measures that may introduce Persecution for Conscience-sake. I have always been a profess'd Advocate for Liberty, both Civil and Religious, as the only rational Foundation of Society, and I trust that no Station of Life will ever alter my Sentiments. Religion, where its Principles are not destructive to civil Society, is to be judged of by HIM only who is the Searcher of all Hearts, and I think it is as unreasonable to perfecute Men for their Religious Opinions as for their Faces: But as the World is now circumstanced, no Purity of Heart, no Set of religious Principles will protect us from an Enemy. Were we even to content ourselves with Cottages, and the spontaneous Productions of Nature, they would rob us of the very Soil: But where Treasure is, they will be eager and watchful to break in and Spoil us of it. You yourselves have seen the Necessity of acting in civil Affairs as Jurymen and Judges, to convict and condemn such little Rogues to Death as break into your Houses, and of acting in other Offices, where Force must necessarily be used for the Preservation of the publick Peace. And are the Fruits of your Labour, and the Labour of your Forefathers reserved only to be given up all at once to his Majesty's Enemies, and the Enemies of your Religion and Liberties? The Freeholders of the Province have chosen you for their Representatives, and many of the principal Inhabitants have publickly petitioned you, that some Measures may be taken for the Defence of the Country: Where then will be the Inconsistency or Partiality of complying with what I have recommended and they have desired? Whatever Expence it shall be attended with, they will with Reason expect you shall bear your Proportion of it, as was done here in the Sum granted to Queen *Anne* for reducing *Canada,* and as has always been done by Men of the same religious Persuasions in *Britain* for carrying on a War against the publick Enemy; but none of them I believe are so unreasonable as to expect, that such as are principled against bearing Arms shall be compelled to act, or be punished for not acting, against their Consciences. Thus I am instructed by your Proprietors, in a manner most affectionate to you, to guard you from, and this I perfectly agreeable to my own Inclinations.

A Mind employed as mine has been about the Defence of the Province, has long since made it self acquainted with.

Franklin also took pride in keeping the printing clean, sharp, and free from smears. The differences between the *Pennsylvania Gazette* and its competitor were clear for everyone to see. It didn't take long for community leaders to notice and pass on the word to others. In time, Franklin's print shop became the official printer for Pennsylvania,

Delaware, and New Jersey. Franklin printed documents, laws, treaties, and paper money for each of these colonies.

In addition to publishing the newspaper and running the printing business, Franklin and Meredith also sold paper, ink, and other goods. The business thrived, thanks in large part to the 12- to 15-hour days Franklin was working, which didn't go unnoticed.

"The industry of Franklin is superior to anything I ever saw of the kind," said Patrick Baird, a Philadelphia physician. Baird continued, "I see him still at work when I go home, and he is at work again before his neighbors are out of bed."

While Franklin seemed cut out for the printing business, Meredith found it wasn't what he wanted to do with his life. Franklin understood. In 1730, with the financial help of two of his friends from Junto, Franklin bought the business from Meredith, who decided he would be happier working on his father's farm.

Word also came that Deborah Read's husband had died, and Franklin was eager to have another chance to marry his "Debby." However, some complications remained. Sometime in 1729 or 1730, Franklin had fathered a son, William Temple Franklin. Franklin never married William's mother, and historians don't know her name. Franklin had chosen to raise his son on his own.

Nevertheless, on September 1, 1730, Franklin married Deborah Read. She proved to be a good match for Franklin. She worked in his shop and helped raise William. She treated William as if he were her own son.

It didn't take long for the little family to grow. A son, Francis, arrived in 1732. At the same time, Franklin's career was growing more and more successful. His *Pennsylvania Gazette* became the leading newspaper of Philadelphia. In time, Franklin published several newspapers in the colonies as well as in the islands of Jamaica and Antigua. Not all the newspapers made money, but that wasn't really important to Franklin. He was more interested in making sure people could have inexpensive reading material. He never forgot his younger days when he had to save his pennies to buy books and collect candle stubs to read by at night.

Franklin's business also published books on home medicine. The books were important because many people lived in remote areas of the colonies far from any doctors.

In 1732, Franklin also began publishing *Poor Richard's Almanack*, a witty collection of advice, humor, and useful facts. In addition, the almanac included predictions on the weather and other events that would happen in the coming year.

While other publishers printed almanacs as a way to fill time when business was slow, Franklin

BY DILIGENCE AND PERSEVERANCE THE MOUSE EAT THE CABLE IN TWO

DILIGENCE IS THE MOTHER OF GOOD LUCK; AND GOD GIVES ALL THINGS TO INDUSTRY

This illustration from Franklin's almanac shows that steady work eventually gets the job done.

knew an almanac could make money if it entertained its readers. He also knew most people didn't believe anyone could actually predict the future with much accuracy, so Ben vowed to make the predictions amusing.

Richard Saunders, or "Poor Richard," made the predictions each year. According to the introduction of the almanac, Poor Richard was writing an almanac because his wife threatened to burn all his books and scientific instruments if he didn't do something useful with them. Other publishers often used psychics to make predictions, but Richard Saunders made them himself. In fact,

> *Much of the success of Poor Richard's Almanack came from the fact that people loved the clever proverbs. Some of the proverbs printed in the almanac through the years included:*
>
> *He's a fool that makes his doctor his heir.*
>
> *Fish and visitors smell in three days.*
>
> *The worst wheel of a cart makes the most noise.*

Richard Saunders was actually Benjamin Franklin.

Franklin's strategy worked. People loved it! *Poor Richard's Almanack* became so successful that Franklin continued to publish a new almanac every year for 25 years. Each year, about 10,000 readers eagerly awaited its arrival.

As Franklin enjoyed more success, he took on a greater role in Philadelphia's public life. Because he loved reading so much, Franklin's first project was starting a subscription library in his community. Junto members often shared their books, but Franklin wanted to share the joy of reading with more than just his small group.

Under Franklin's plan for a larger library, subscribers would pay a fee to buy the library's first books and get it going. Subscribers would then pay yearly dues that would be used to buy more books. The library would be open once a week to subscribers. If a subscriber didn't return a book when it was due, he or she would pay double the value of the book as a fine.

In 1731 when Franklin launched his project, few people in Philadelphia were readers. Most didn't have money to spend on books. Franklin started the library with just 50 subscribers, but that number doubled within 11 years.

Franklin's Library Company of Philadelphia was the first of its kind in North America. Other communities copied the idea and started libraries of their own. Soon, reading became a popular pastime in the colonies. Franklin later wrote in his autobiography,

Franklin organized a subscription library in order to share his love of reading with his community.

These libraries have improved the general conversation of

When trying to gain subscribers for the library, Franklin discovered it was best to be humble. People shied away from subscribing when they thought Franklin was setting up the library for his own glory. So he decided to take another approach. He told potential subscribers that his friends were organizing a library project and had asked him to collect donations from others who loved to read. Using this approach, Franklin had no problem finding subscribers to get the project started. He would use this tactic again and again, choosing to stay behind the scenes rather than take credit for his ideas.

the Americans, made the common tradesmen and farmers as intelligent as most gentlemen from other countries, and perhaps have contributed in some degree to the stand so generally made throughout the Colonies in defense of their privileges.

Most of his life, Franklin saved an hour or two each day to educate himself. He studied French, Latin, Spanish, and other languages. He read just about everything he could get his hands on. Franklin felt this daily studying helped make up for the education he didn't get as a child.

Because education remained a high priority for him, Franklin believed Philadelphia should start its own college. Students could then continue their studies in Philadelphia rather than having to go to other cities. In 1751, Franklin founded a school that became the University of Pennsylvania. He especially enjoyed seeing students take what they learned in college and use it to benefit others by going into public serv-

In addition to the Union Fire Company, Franklin organized a fire insurance company in Philadelphia.

ice. He felt public service ranked as one of the most important things a person could do.

In 1737, Franklin became deputy postmaster for Philadelphia. The year before, he had helped start Philadelphia's Union Fire Company. This group was formed because of an essay he wrote for a Junto meeting about ways people could avoid fires caused by accidents or carelessness. This essay was published in the newspaper and drew a great deal of attention.

People talked about Franklin's article and decided to form a firefighting group. About 30 people joined what became the Union Fire Company. Each member agreed to keep leather buckets and baskets handy. When a house fire blazed, members brought buckets of water to put out the blaze and baskets to save whatever household goods they could.

The group met once a month to discuss fires that had occurred and come up with better ideas for preventing and fighting them. As others in the community saw the effectiveness of the group, firefighting companies popped up across the community. Eventually, just about every man in Philadelphia who owned property joined a group.

Franklin's quest for safety didn't end with starting a fire department. In the 1740s, when England and France were fighting King George's War, Franklin helped

Franklin lived simply. He didn't wear flashy clothing or buy many fancy things. Because of his thrift, he was able to retire at a young age and still live comfortably. It surprised him to see how others spent their money. For instance, when Franklin visited one of his wealthy friends, he asked his friend why his home had such huge rooms. His friend replied that he could afford it. Franklin replied with a grin, "Why don't you buy a hat six times too big for your head? You can afford that, too."

organize a militia to defend Philadelphia against a possible French attack. In 1745, he also helped create a city police force.

Franklin was becoming a wealthy man. By 1745, he earned more than 2,000 pounds a year. In those days, an ordinary working man considered himself fortunate to earn about 15 pounds a year. By 1748, Franklin had gained enough wealth to retire from the printing business, even though he was just 42 years old. He reached a partnership agreement with David Hall, one of his trusted employees. The agreement left Franklin free for other activities while providing him an income. Hall would run the business for 20 years and pay Franklin half the profits. After that, Hall could call the business his own.

Many people thought it odd that Franklin would leave such a successful business. Had he stayed, he could have become one of the richest men in the colonies. Wealth, however, wasn't important to Franklin. He had better things to do with his time than make more money than he would ever spend.

"I would rather have it said, he lived usefully, than, he died rich," Franklin wrote to his mother. Franklin was not interested in spending his retirement in leisure. He planned to devote his time to science. ❧

6 MAN OF SCIENCE

‿❦‿

All his life Franklin had been curious about the way things worked. He often tinkered with things to make them work better. In the 1740s, he began working on a better way to heat rooms.

At the time, wood-burning fireplaces and stoves were the main source of heat in buildings. As Philadelphia grew, however, firewood became more scarce and more expensive. Franklin wanted to build a better fireplace—one that used less wood but still heated a room well. His solution was called the Franklin stove or the Philadelphia fireplace.

"My common room I know is made twice as warm as it used to be, with a quarter of the wood I formerly used," Franklin wrote about his invention. The Franklin stove worked so well that it became

In this painting by Benjamin West, Franklin draws electricity from the sky.

popular throughout the colonies. "The use of these fireplaces in very many houses both of this and the neighboring colonies has been, and is, a great saving of wood to the inhabitants," Franklin continued.

The Franklin stove is just one example of Benjamin Franklin's inventiveness. He invented many other things as well, including improvements to the printing press, a chair that could be converted into a ladder, and a new kind of candle. This candle, made of whale oil, produced a brighter light and lasted longer than ordinary candles.

Franklin also invented a musical instrument called the glass harmonica. This instrument looked like a piano, but instead of pressing keys, the musician would touch his or her fingers against a set of spinning crystal cups. The instrument became very popular, and composers such as Mozart and Beethoven wrote pieces for the glass harmonica. Like many early instruments, however, it is no longer very commonly used.

Another Franklin invention, however, can be seen today on the noses of people everywhere. Franklin invented bifocal eyeglasses. The lenses of these eyglasses were split in half, with each half ground to a different prescription. Franklin wrote, "I have only to move my Eyes up or down, as I want to see distinctly far or near."

Friends suggested that Franklin patent his inventions and get paid for them. He said he wanted

In this illustration, Franklin plays his glass harmonica by touching his fingers to rotating crystal glasses.

the world to benefit from his inventions, but he didn't need to profit from them. He wrote,

> *That, as we enjoy great advantages from the inventions of others, we should be glad of an opportunity to serve others by any invention of ours; and this we should do freely and generously.*

While Franklin chose to be generous with his creations, other people weren't so considerate. Without the protection of a patent, Franklin's inventions could be copied by others who could then get patents themselves. In one instance, a London man copied the Franklin stove and made a fortune.

Though they didn't make him money, Franklin's inventions did make him famous. But Franklin's experiments with electricity made him known around the world.

Franklin became interested in experimenting with electricity after hearing a lecture by Scottish scientist Dr. Archibald Spencer in Boston. He wrote his friend Peter Collinson, "I never was before engaged in any study that so totally engrossed my attention and my time as this has lately done." Collinson lived in London and was a member of Britain's Royal Society, the most important scientific group in Britain.

At this time, not much was known about electricity. Scientists had many theories about this strange force, but Franklin wanted to learn from his own observations. Soon Franklin had converted a room in his home into a workshop where he could test some of his own ideas about electricity. His son William and daughter Sarah, born in 1743, would often help or quietly watch. Franklin's wife looked at the room filled with jars, tools, and bits of metal, glass, and other items and just shook her head. She saw a cluttered mess, but Franklin saw something much more.

Franklin also used the world as his laboratory. He had observed lightning in the sky and noted its similarities to sparks of electricity. As a result of his work, Franklin invented the lightning rod, a device to protect buildings from damage by lightning strikes. Lightning rods soon appeared on buildings in Philadelphia and around the world.

Franklin used these models in his experiments with lightning rods.

In 1750, he published a book, *Experiments and Observations on Electricity,* in which he explained his ideas and suggested experiments. This book was translated into German, Italian, and French and brought Franklin great fame throughout Europe.

Yet Franklin still wanted to prove that lightning

In this famous experiment, his son William watches as Franklin shows that lightning is electricity.

was made up of electricity. One day in 1752, he sent up a kite into a stormy sky. Attached to the kite's string was a metal key. When storm clouds passed overhead, the electricity in the clouds made the loose threads on the kite string stand up. When Ben touched the key, he felt a jolt of electricity. Electricity had followed the kite string and passed from the key to

Franklin enjoyed entertaining his friends with electrical tricks. One of his favorites involved taking a piece of wire with many "legs," running an electrical current through it, and making it walk like a spider.

his finger. The experiment was very dangerous, but it demonstrated the clouds that produce lightning contain electricity.

This kite experiment was just one of many attempts Franklin made to better understand this strange force. He became known as a pioneer in the new scientific field of electricity. His scientific interests, however, were varied. In 1736, when his 4-year-old son Francis died of smallpox, Franklin began to study diseases. He learned about the spread of disease and studied the new, experimental practice of inoculation. He also studied sunspots, magnets, and the communication of ants. He helped farmers by showing them that acidic soil can be improved by adding a substance called lime. He was the first to study the Gulf Stream, the current that runs through the Atlantic Ocean.

The creativity that made Franklin so successful as a scientist and inventor helped him in other ways as well. Once, when traveling, he stopped at a tavern. All he wanted to do was warm himself in front of the fire, but he quickly discovered that many others had the same idea. How could he get close enough to the fire to warm up? Franklin asked the tavern owner's son to take a quart of oysters out to his horse. Curious about the oyster-eating horse, the other people in the tavern followed the boy outside. When the horse refused to touch the oysters, everyone went back inside. They found Franklin sitting comfortably in front of the fire.

In 1753, both Harvard and Yale colleges honored Franklin for his scientific achievements. Later that year, Britain's Royal Society awarded him its highest honor, the Copley Gold Medal, for his work as a scientist. In 1756, the College of William and Mary granted him an honorary degree, and in 1772, he was elected to the French Academy of Sciences.

Although Franklin had just two years of formal schooling, he received so many awards and honorary degrees that people began to call him Dr. Franklin.

Despite his many inventions, discoveries, and honors, Franklin wanted to learn more. He knew even greater inventions were to come, and he wished he could see into the future. In 1780, he wrote to a friend,

The rapid progress true Science now makes occasions my regretting sometimes that I was born too soon. It is impossible to imagine the Heights to which may be carried, in a thousand years, the Power of Man over

The Copley Gold Medal, awarded by Britain's Royal Society, is similar to today's Nobel Prize.

Matter. We may perhaps learn to deprive large Masses of their Gravity, and give them absolute Levity, for the sake of very easy transport. Agriculture may diminish its Labour and double its Produce; all Diseases may, by sure means, be prevented or cured, not even excepting that of Old Age, and our Lives lengthened at pleasure.

Even in his old age, Franklin continued to discover and invent. In his later years, he invented a device to grab items from high places, a chair with a built-in fan, and a tool that copied his letters as he was writing them. ❧

7 POLITICS

❧❦❧

As Franklin's fame as a scientist grew, he also became active in politics. He was elected to the Philadelphia Common Council in 1748, his first elected public office. In 1753, he was named deputy postmaster for Britain's North American colonies, and he worked to make mail delivery faster and more reliable.

With the start of the French and Indian War in 1754, England and France were once again at odds. Franklin played a leading role in defending Pennsylvania against attacks by France's Native American allies. He was elected a colonel in the Pennsylvania militia, and he helped plan a series of new forts in western Pennsylvania. He also was instrumental in arranging for supplies for British troops who used Pennsylvania as their base.

Benjamin Franklin was active in Pennsylvania political life, as well as that of the colonies. He wrote many papers and made numerous proposals on behalf of his emerging nation.

Franklin urged the colonies to unite to help defend one another. He represented Pennsylvania at a meeting of seven British colonies held at Albany, New York. At the meeting, Franklin proposed a plan for the colonies to unite and be governed by a president and a grand council. His plan, however, was rejected. The individual colonies were not ready to give up power to a new central government.

In 1757, the Pennsylvania assembly appointed Franklin to serve as its representative in England. He would have to move to London. "In two years at farthest I hope to settle all my affairs in such a manner, as that I may then conveniently remove to England, provided we can persuade the good woman to cross the seas," Franklin wrote in a letter to an English friend.

Franklin took his son, William, with him to England in 1757. They traveled throughout Europe, including Scotland, Belgium, and Holland. They also visited relatives in Ecton, England, where Franklin's father had lived before moving to the colonies in 1683.

The "good woman" Franklin wrote about was his wife, Deborah, who was terrified of ships and water. Fearing a long and hazardous sea journey, she wouldn't consider moving. As it turned out, Franklin and Deborah spent most of the rest of their married life apart from each other. He remained in England for much of the next two decades.

While Franklin was away, relations between Great Britain and its American colonies grew strained. Great Britain had gained vast new territories in North America through its war with France. The war, however, also drained British funds. To pay for the war effort, the British government introduced new taxes on its American colonies. Those taxes were met with howls of protest from American colonists who claimed that Parliament had no right to tax them without their approval.

One set of taxes, known as the Stamp Act, particularly angered colonists. The Stamp Act taxed marriage licenses, newspapers, wills, and other

Colonists protested the new taxes of the Stamp Act by burning royal stamps in a bonfire.

common documents. Each document was required to carry a royal stamp, which the government sold.

Franklin warned Britain's lawmakers that the Stamp Act would anger the colonists, but they ignored him. Yet Britain couldn't ignore the riots that broke out in New York City and Boston as a result of these new taxes. Franklin spent nearly every moment of his day talking to British lawmakers and getting letters from the colonies about the Stamp Act printed in British newspapers. The colonists even signed agreements not to buy products from England until the Stamp Act was repealed.

On February 13, 1766, Franklin appeared before Parliament and gave a heartfelt speech. He detailed the taxes the colonists already paid and refuted claims that all colonists were rich. He explained that colonists living in remote areas couldn't get married or write wills because they had to travel so far and pay so much money to get a royal stamp.

His speech also carried a warning. The colonies' population continued to grow. With 300,000 able-bodied men already living in the colonies, a rather impressive army could be formed if they chose to fight. Even if things didn't go that far, the colonies could hurt Great Britain economically by refusing to purchase its goods.

Franklin ended his speech by saying the consequences of not repealing the Stamp Act could be costly to Britain. The result could be "a total loss of the respect and affection the people of America bear this country, and of all the commerce that depends on that respect and affection," he said.

The following week, the Stamp Act was repealed. Newspapers in nearly every colony printed Franklin's speech. His popularity soared in the colonies.

The British government soon imposed new taxes on the colonists, however, and this time Franklin could not stop them. The new taxes prompted new protests in Boston and other colonial cities. In 1773, a Boston mob protested the new tax on tea by destroying thousands of pounds of tea

Franklin appeared before Britain's Parliament to argue against the Stamp Act.

waiting to be unloaded from a ship in Boston Harbor. The event later came to be called the Boston Tea Party, and it alarmed the British government in London. The protests grew into riots. The British government looked for someone to blame for the disorder in the colonies. They settled on the most prominent American in England: Benjamin Franklin.

British leaders accused Franklin of encouraging the disorderly protest. Members of the British government gave him a humiliating public scolding. To punish him for his support of the patriots, the government also dismissed Franklin from his job as deputy postmaster. Clearly he would no longer be a useful agent in England. It was time for him to return to Philadelphia.

Sadly, his return came too late for Deborah Franklin. She had continued to live in Philadelphia during her husband's long stay in England. She died in 1774 after a long illness.

Franklin returned home to Philadelphia in March of the fol-

For as long as he possibly could, Franklin held on to the hope that war could be avoided between Great Britain and the American colonies. During his last day in London, he sorted through bundles of newspapers that had come from the colonies. He pointed out articles he thought might help the colonists' cause if reprinted in British papers. An English friend who helped Franklin go through the papers later remembered that day and Franklin's sadness: "He was frequently not able to proceed for the tears literally running down his cheeks."

lowing year. His sea voyage to Philadelphia took more than six weeks. While Franklin was at sea, the clashes between Britain and the American colonies intensified until, on April 19, 1775, in Lexington, Massachusetts, a British officer confronted 70 armed American Minutemen. When ordered to disperse, one American responded with a shot.

Deborah Franklin and her husband lived most of their married life on two different continents.

A battle later that day in the nearby town of Concord prompted American writer Ralph Waldo Emerson to compose a poem in which he referred to the Concord militia's collective musket fire as "the shot heard round the world." The American Revolution had begun. ॐ

8 A NEW NATION

❧❀❧

Almost as soon as his ship arrived in Philadelphia, Franklin went to work for the American cause. The day after he returned home, he was selected to represent Pennsylvania in the Second Continental Congress. Later, he was asked to serve as the president of the Committee of Safety, which was planning the defense of Pennsylvania. One of the problems facing the committee was a lack of weapons and ammunition. As usual, Franklin proposed an original and unique solution. He suggested the patriots use bows and arrows, but his suggestion was rejected.

Franklin also established a new post office for the colonies and helped George Washington organize the new army. Franklin's many duties kept him so busy that he wrote to a friend,

Benjamin Franklin helped Thomas Jefferson write the Declaration of Independence..

My time was never more fully employed. In the morning at 6, I am at the committee of safety, appointed by the assembly to put the province in a state of defense; which committee holds till near 9, when I am at the congress, and that sits till after 4 in the afternoon.

Franklin's work in the American Revolution led him to leave behind old friends and even family members who remained loyal to Great Britain. He cut off contact with his son William after his son chose to side with Great Britain. Not long after Franklin returned to Philadelphia, he wrote a letter to an old British friend named William Strahan:

Some of Franklin's political enemies accused him of being a spy during the American Revolution. As proof, they pointed to the fact that he had spent a great deal of time in England and that his son William remained loyal to the British. Of course, the accusations were false.

Mr. Strahan, You are a member of Parliament, and one of that majority which has doomed my country to destruction. ... Look upon your hands! They are stained with the blood of your relations! You and I were long friends. You are now my enemy and I am yours, B. Franklin.

For years, Franklin had worked to preserve peace between Britain and the colonies. Once the war

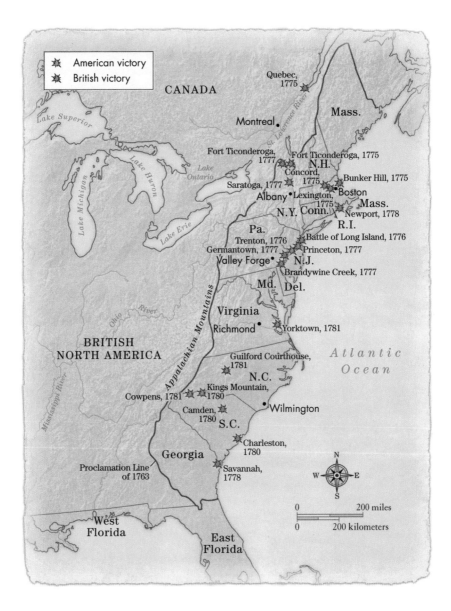

American victory

British victory

CANADA

Lake Superior

Lake Michigan

Lake Huron

Lake Ontario

Lake Erie

Quebec, 1775

Montreal

Mass.

N.H.

Fort Ticonderoga, 1777

Fort Ticonderoga, 1775

Concord, 1775

Bunker Hill, 1775

Saratoga, 1777

Lexington, 1775

Boston

Albany

Mass.

N.Y.

Conn.

Newport, 1778

R.I.

Pa.

Battle of Long Island, 1776

Trenton, 1776

Germantown, 1777

Princeton, 1777

Valley Forge

N.J.

Brandywine Creek, 1777

Md.

Del.

Virginia

Richmond

Yorktown, 1781

BRITISH
NORTH AMERICA

Appalachian Mountains

Ohio River

Guilford Courthouse, 1781

N.C.

Atlantic
Ocean

Kings Mountain, 1780

Cowpens, 1781

Camden, 1780

Wilmington

S.C.

Mississippi River

Charleston, 1780

Georgia

Savannah, 1778

N

W   E

S

Proclamation Line
of 1763

0   200 miles

0   200 kilometers

West
Florida

East
Florida

began, he put aside his old loyalties to Britain. He and Thomas Jefferson, a delegate from Virginia, became two of the strongest voices for American

Major battles of the American Revolution were fought throughout the colonies.

independence. As a member of the Continental Congress, Franklin helped put forward a plan for uniting the colonies as an independent nation. Not everyone in Congress was ready to take that step, however. The war continued for more than a year before Congress finally began considering independence.

In June 1776, Richard Henry Lee of Virginia introduced a resolution for Congress to debate and vote on. It declared that the colonies "are and of right ought to be free and independent states." Congress formed a committee of five members to write a statement explaining to the world why the colonies should be independent. Franklin was selected for the committee, along with Thomas Jefferson, John Adams, Roger Sherman, and Robert Livingston. Jefferson wrote the document, with Franklin and the others helping him by editing his work. On July 4, 1776, Congress voted to accept the Declaration of Independence. Franklin and the other members of Congress signed the document about one month later.

After John Hancock, president of the Congress, signed the declaration, he said, "We must be unanimous, there must be no pulling different ways; we must all hang together." They knew that in the eyes of the British government they were now traitors and could pay with their lives. As often happened, Franklin broke the tension of the

This draft of the Declaration of Independence shows edits made by Franklin and others.

moment with his wit. "Yes," he said, "we must indeed all hang together, or most assuredly we shall all hang separately."

Of course, the Declaration of Independence

would mean little if the new United States could not defeat the mighty British army and navy. To do that, the new nation needed help. Because France had long been a rival of Great Britain, the United States turned to France for money and military support.

Congress chose Franklin to help negotiate an alliance with France. Along with Silas Deane and Arthur Lee, he would go to France to convince the French government to help the United States win its independence. Franklin was now 70 years old, and he faced another difficult sea journey to Europe. This time, there would be the added danger of attack by British warships. "I am old and good for nothing," he complained to a friend. But his new nation needed him.

Franklin took two of his grandsons with him to France: Temple Franklin, William's son, and Benjamin "Benny" Bache, Sarah's son. Instead of supporting Great Britain like his father did, Temple was on the side of his grandfather when the Revolutionary War broke out. In France, Temple assisted his aging grandfather and helped care for Benny, who turned 7 before the trio left for France.

As it turned out, Franklin played an important role in winning French support. His fame as a scientist, inventor, and diplomat had spread to France. To the French people, he was the most famous of all Americans. In fact, they saw him as a symbol of the new United States.

Franklin settled in the small town of Passy, just outside Paris.

In his plain clothes, glasses, and fur hat, Franklin was easy to recognize on the streets of Paris. Compared to French diplomats and royalty, Franklin's manner and dress were a refreshing change of pace. He was such a popular figure that paintings and images of him sold quickly in France. Even dolls were created to resemble him. Women created a new hairstyle based on Franklin's fur hat. They called it *Coiffure à la Franklin*.

Benjamin Franklin was a frequent and popular visitor to the French court.

Franklin used this goodwill to secure French support for the American Revolution. The French were uncertain if it was wise to form an alliance with the American colonies, since doing so would mean war with Britain. Nevertheless, with patience and skillful diplomacy, Franklin convinced France to enter into a formal alliance with the United States. France publicly announced the alliance on March 20, 1778. Now, along with sending weapons and ammunition, France would send an army and a fleet of warships to fight alongside the Americans against Great Britain.

France's support was vital to the success of the American Revolution. In 1781, French troops helped George Washington's Continental Army trap the British army at Yorktown, Virginia. Surrounded by Washington and his French allies, the British surrendered on October 16, 1781. The United States had won its independence.

Now an old man and still living in France, Franklin had asked Congress three times in five years to release him from his overseas duty. In March 1781, Franklin wrote:

> *I have passed my seventy-fifth year, and I find that the long and severe fit of the gout which I had the last winter has shaken me exceedingly, and I am yet far from having recovered the bodily strength I before enjoyed. And as I can not at present undergo the fatigues of a sea voyage (the last having been too much for me) and*

would not again expose myself to the hazard of capture and imprisonment in this time of war, I purpose to remain here at least 'till the peace; perhaps may be for the remainder of my life; and if any knowledge or experience I have acquired here may be thought of use to my successor, I shall freely communicate it, and assist him with any influence I may be supposed to have, or counsel that may be desired of me.

After the siege of Yorktown, the British surrendered, bringing an end to the war.

81

This painting by Benjamin West shows the men who represented the United States in the Treaty of Paris: from left, John Jay, John Adams, Benjamin Franklin, Henry Laurens, and Temple Franklin, the delegation's secretary. The British diplomats refused to pose, and so the painting was never finished.

However, with the war's end, Congress insisted Franklin continue his work. He represented the United States in negotiating a peace treaty with Great Britain. Franklin and other diplomats signed the treaty in Paris in 1783. In the treaty, Great Britain accepted that their former colonies were now free, sovereign, and independent. The treaty also established the borders of the new country.

"We are now friends with England and with all mankind," Franklin wrote to his friend Josiah Quincy.

He continued, "May we never see another war! For in my opinion there never was a good war or a bad peace."

Although while in France Franklin worked tirelessly for the American cause, he enjoyed a rich social life. He dined at fine restaurants and enjoyed playing chess with friends. He also enjoyed many flirtations. One woman, a French widow named Madame Helvétius, was a special favorite. He proposed marriage, but she refused him.

> *John Adams, one of the diplomats who signed the Treaty of Paris ending the Revolutionary War, would go on to become the second president of the new United States of America.*

During his last two years in France, Franklin found more time to devote to science. In 1782, he watched with fascination as balloons were developed. The balloons were usually filled with heated air or hydrogen and could carry roosters, ducks, or sheep in baskets hanging below. Franklin saw many possibilities for the invention if the balloon's basket could carry people. He wrote to an English friend,

> *This discovery might possibly give a new turn to human affairs. Convincing sovereigns of the folly of wars may perhaps be one effect of it, since it will be impossible for the most potent of them to guard his dominions. Five thousand balloons, capable of raising two men each,*

could not cost more than five ships, and where is the prince who can afford to cover his country with troops for defense, so that ten thousand men descending from the clouds might not in many places do an infinite deal of mischief before a force could be brought together to defend them?

After seeing a demonstration of this new invention, an aquaintance asked Franklin, "What good is it?" Franklin responded, "What good is a newborn child?"

Despite his fascination with life in France, Franklin was ready to come home when his country allowed it. In 1785, the Continental Congress passed a resolution releasing Franklin from duty in France. Worried about Franklin's health, his friends urged him to live out the rest of his life in France rather than risk another ocean voyage. "I want to die in my own country," he said in reply.

After Franklin's departure, Thomas Jefferson was appointed the new ambassador to France. When asked if he was Franklin's replacement, Jefferson responded that no one could replace him. Jefferson would later be elected the third president of the United States.

Now 79 years old and weak from illness, Franklin embarked on his final ocean voyage. He left France on June 12, 1785, and nearly everyone in Passy turned out to bid him farewell.

When Benjamin Franklin arrived in Philadelphia

on September 14, 1785, he was carried down Market Street. As he passed, a joyous crowd cheered and church bells rang to honor him. Sixty-two years had passed since Benjamin Franklin had first walked down Market Street as a poor and homeless young man. Now he returned in triumph to the new nation he helped to create. ℘

When Franklin returned to Philadelphia from France, he was carried down the streets by an excited and grateful crowd.

9 THE FINAL YEARS

Chapter

❧❧❧

In his diary, Franklin rejoiced at returning to his "dear Philadelphia." Best of all, he was reunited with his family. He lived with his daughter, Sarah, and spent time with his grandchildren. In their house, he built a new library to hold the thousands of books and scientific instruments he had collected over the years. He was happy to find his family in good health and circumstances.

Not all of Franklin's family was together in Philadelphia, though. His son William remained in England. The relationship between Franklin and William remained difficult after William sided with Britain in the American Revolution.

Troubles remained for the new United States as well. In 1781, the 13 states had united under the

This statue of Benjamin Franklin stands outside Boston's Old City Hall and is one of the sites on that city's famous Freedom Trail.

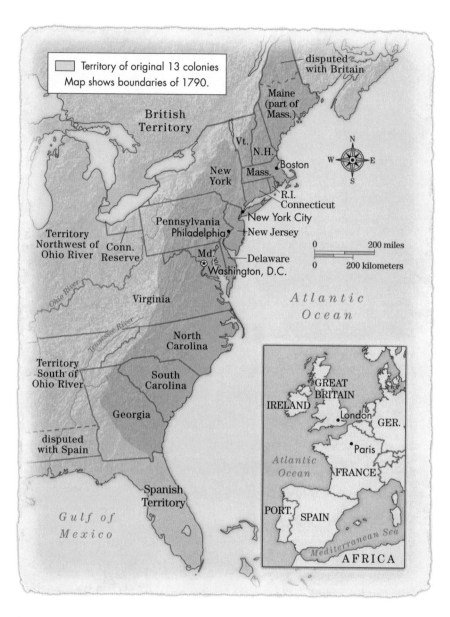

Territory of original 13 colonies
Map shows boundaries of 1790.

disputed
with Britain

Maine
(part of
Mass.)

British
Territory

Vt.

N.H.

Boston

New
York

Mass.

R.I.

Connecticut

Pennsylvania

New York City

Philadelphia

New Jersey

Territory
Northwest of
Ohio River

Conn.
Reserve

Md.

Delaware

Washington, D.C.

Virginia

*Atlantic
Ocean*

North
Carolina

Territory
South of
Ohio River

South
Carolina

Georgia

disputed
with Spain

Spanish
Territory

*Gulf of
Mexico*

0   200 miles
0   200 kilometers

Ohio River

Tennessee River

GREAT
BRITAIN

IRELAND

London

GER.

Paris

*Atlantic
Ocean*

FRANCE

PORT.

SPAIN

Mediterranean Sea

AFRICA

Although Franklin spent much of his adult life in Europe, he considered Philadelphia his home.

Articles of Confederation, but the union of states was a fragile one. The states argued about debts, borders, and other issues. The new Congress had little power to solve the problems facing the nation.

On May 2, 1787, a national convention opened to form a new plan of government. The Constitutional Convention met in Philadelphia, and Franklin served as one of Pennsylvania's delegates. At 82 years old, he was the oldest member of the convention. Five days a week, he walked nearly half a mile to the State House where the convention met. He never missed a session.

When arguments between delegates threatened to sink the convention, Franklin stepped forward. One of the big problems the delegates faced was how to settle differences between larger and smaller states. The smaller states wanted as many representatives in the new government as the larger states. Delegates from the larger states argued that this wouldn't be fair. Franklin proposed an important compromise that allowed the convention's work to continue. Franklin suggested that each state be equally represented in one house of Congress, today called the Senate. In the second house, today known as the House of Representatives,

When he returned to Philadelphia, Franklin added on to his house to make it more comfortable for Sarah and her family. Because they often entertained guests, he decided to add a dining room with a table that seated 24 people. The addition to his library made his personal space more orderly. At the time, Franklin had the largest private library in the entire United States.

states could be represented based on population. He helped push through the compromise, one of many made during the four-month convention.

With so many compromises, different pieces of the final Constitution pleased few of the delegates. Franklin knew getting the Constitution passed unanimously was vital. The new country had to stand united. Franklin passionately appealed to the delegates to set aside their differences, approve the Constitution unanimously, and present a united front when urging passage of the document in their states. Franklin told the delegates,

Benjamin Franklin and other members of the Constitutional Convention worked to create a plan for governing their new country.

I confess there are several parts of the Constitution which I do not at present approve; but, Sir, I am not sure I shall never approve them; for, having lived long, I have experienced many instances of being obliged, by better information or fuller consideration, to change opinions, even on important subjects, which I once thought right, but found to be otherwise. Thus I consent, Sir, to this Constitution, because I expect no better, and because I am not sure that it is not the best.

The U.S. Constitution was approved and signed by Franklin and the other members of the convention on September 17, 1787. After winning approval by the states, the Constitution took effect on March 4, 1789.

Meanwhile, Franklin retired from public life to work on his autobiography, which he had begun years earlier in an attempt to teach his son the lessons he had learned in his active lifetime. He continued to write letters and

After the Constitutional Convention, Franklin held one more office— the presidency of the Pennsylvania Society for Promoting the Abolition of Slavery, and the Relief of Free Negroes Unlawfully Held in Bondage. Although Franklin had owned several slaves many years earlier, he began speaking out against slavery as early as 1751. As president of the nation's first abolition society, Franklin penned letters to the governors of several Northern states and shamed them for letting merchants and shipping crews participate in the slave trade.

play cards with friends and family for as long as his health allowed. He wrote to an English friend,

> *The companions of my youth are indeed almost all departed, but I find an agreeable society among their children and grandchildren. Considering our well-furnished, plentiful market as the best of gardens, I am turning mine, in the midst of which my house stands, into grass plots and gravel walks, with trees and flowering shrubs. Cards we some-times play here, in long winter evenings.*

In January 1788, Franklin fell on the stone steps in his garden and injured his wrist and arm. Walking became increasingly difficult for him, and he suffered great pain from a kidney stone. He remained in bed for much of his final years of life.

On April 10, 1790, Franklin had another bout of pleurisy. He no longer had the strength to fight it. Benjamin Franklin died quietly at 11 P.M. on April 17, 1790, with his favorite grandsons, Temple and Benny, at his bedside. He was 84 years old.

He was buried next to his wife, Deborah, at Christ Church Cemetery in Philadelphia. More than 20,000 people attended his funeral. It was the largest crowd to gather in Philadelphia up to that time.

At age 22, Franklin had written what he then thought he wanted on his tombstone:

Benjamin Franklin is known as a founding father of the United States of America.

The Body of
B. Franklin,
Printer;
Like the Cover of an old Book,
Its contents torn out,
And script of its Lettering and Gilding,
Lies here, Food for Worms.
But the Work shall not be wholly lost,
For it will, as he believed, appear once more,
In a new & more perfect Edition,
Corrected and amended
By the Author.

In his final will, however, he chose a simpler statement for the headstone at his and Deborah's grave: "Benjamin and Deborah Franklin 1790."

In the United States, the House of Representatives passed a resolution mourning Franklin's death. So did the National Assembly of France, which remembered Franklin for his achievements as a diplomat and as a scientist.

And yet Franklin was so much more. As he wrote in *Poor Richard's Almanack* of 1738,

> *If you wou'd not be forgotten*
> *As soon as you are dead and rotten*
> *Either write things worth reading,*
> *Or do things worth the writing.*

Benjamin Franklin did both. His autobiography tells the story of a life well-lived. Franklin was a skilled printer and clever businessman. He was a brilliant scientist and inventor. He organized North America's first subscription library and created Philadelphia's police force and fire department. He was a skillful diplomat and a capable writer. But perhaps most impressive, Benjamin Franklin was the only man to have signed all four early documents most important to the United States of America: the Declaration of Independence, the treaty with France that helped his country win the

Revolution, the treaty with Britain that ended the war, and the U.S. Constitution.

Perhaps the French National Assembly summed it up best when it named Benjamin Franklin "the genius who freed America." ❧

FRANKLIN'S LIFE

1718

Begins serving as apprentice to half brother James

1706

Born on January 17 in Boston

1705

1715

1719

French scientist Rene de Reaumur proposes using wood to make paper, which had previously been made from old cloth

1707

The Act of Union joins Scotland, England, and Wales into the United Kingdom of Great Britain

WORLD EVENTS

1723

Leaves Boston to
begin new life in
Philadelphia

1730

Marries
Deborah Read

1720

Japan lifts ban on
Western literature,
allowing new ideas to
reach the island

1726

Jonathan Swift
publishes *Gulliver's
Travels*

FRANKLIN'S LIFE

1732

Publishes first
annual *Poor
Richard's Almanack*

1752

Conducts experiment
with kite to prove
that lightning is made
of electricity

1750

1749

German writer
Johann Wolfgang
von Goethe is born

1738

Englishman John
Wesley and his brother
Charles found the
Methodist church

WORLD EVENTS

1775

Returns to Philadelphia and is elected to Second Continental Congress

1757

Moves to London to serve as representative of Pennsylvania Assembly in England

1764

James Hargreaves creates the spinning jenny, a mechanical spinning wheel

1774

King Louis XV of France dies and his grandson, Louis XVI is crowned

FRANKLIN'S LIFE

1776

Signs Declaration
of Independence;
serves as American
commissioner
to France

1778

Negotiates alliance
with France to help
United States fight
Great Britain

1775

1776

Scottish economist
Adam Smith pub-
lishes *The Wealth
of Nations*, herald-
ing the beginning of
modern economics

1779

Jan Ingenhousz of the
Netherlands discovers
that plants release
oxygen when exposed
to sunlight

WORLD EVENTS

1782

Negotiates peace treaty with Great Britain to mark end of American Revolution

1790

Dies in Philadelphia on April 17

1788

The *Times* newspaper in London is founded

1783

The first manned hot air balloon flight is made in Paris, France, by the Montgolfier brothers

DATE OF BIRTH: January 17, 1706

BIRTHPLACE: Boston, Massachussetts

FATHER: Josiah Franklin

MOTHER: Abiah Folger Franklin

EDUCATION: Two years in Boston grammar schools

SPOUSE: Deborah Read Franklin (1708–1774)

DATE OF MARRIAGE: September 1730

CHILDREN: William Temple Franklin (1729 or 1730–1813) Francis Folger Franklin (1732–1736) Sarah Franklin Bache (1743–1808)

DATE OF DEATH: April 17, 1790

PLACE OF BURIAL: Philadelphia, Pennsylvania

IN THE LIBRARY

Burke, Rick. *Benjamin Franklin*. Chicago: Heinemann Library, 2003.

Fleming, Candace. *Ben Franklin's Almanac: Being a True Account of the Good Gentleman's Life*. New York: Atheneum, 2003.

Gregson, Susan. *Benjamin Franklin*. Mankato, Minn.: Capstone Press, 2002.

Meltzer, Milton. *Benjamin Franklin: The New American*. New York: Franklin Watts, 1989.

Roop, Connie, and Peter Roop. *Benjamin Franklin*. New York: Scholastic Reference, 2001.

On the Web

For more information on *Benjamin Franklin,* use FactHound to track down Web sites related to this book.

1. Go to *www.facthound.com*
2. Type in a search word related to this book or this book ID: 0756508266
3. Click on the *Fetch It* button.

FactHound will find the best Web sites for you.

Historic Sites

Benjamin Franklin National Memorial
222 N. 20th St.
Philadelphia, PA 19103
215/448-1200
Housed in the Franklin Institute Science Museum, the memorial includes a large marble statue of Franklin and an exhibit hall

Franklin Court on Market Street
Contact: Independence National Historic Park
143 S. Third St.
Philadelphia, PA 19106
215/965-2305
Site of a former Franklin home, now home to an underground museum focusing on Franklin's life and times

abolition
the act of ending or stopping something

arbitrator
one who works to settle disagreements

Articles of Confederation
the 1781 agreement that created a federal government for the new United States of America

autobiography
the story of a person's life written by that person

Constitutional Convention
the group organized to write the U.S. Constitution, the document that states the country's basic laws

diplomats
people whose job is to handle relations between their country and other countries

indentured
working for another for an agreed-upon time period

inoculation
the injection of a substance into a person's body to protect against disease

militia
a loosely organized military group of people

Parliament
the part of the British government that makes laws

pleurisy
an inflammation of the membrane that lines the chest and covers the lungs

Second Continental Congress
a group of American colonists who established laws and addressed problems with the British

smallpox
a disease that causes chills, high fever, and pimples

Chapter 2

Page 14, line 11: H.W. Brands. *The First American: The Life and Times of Benjamin Franklin.* New York: Doubleday, 2000, pp. 15–16.

Page 17, line 4: Eulalie Osgood Grover. *Benjamin Franklin: The Story of Poor Richard.* New York: Dodd, Mead, 1953, p. 7.

Chapter 3

Page 23, line 20: Benjamin Franklin. *The Autobiography of Benjamin Franklin.* New York: Random House, 1944, p. 30.

Chapter 4

Page 30, sidebar: Ibid., p. 37.

Page 31, line 22: Ibid.

Page 32, line 5: Ibid.

Page 35, line 21: Thomas Fleming. *Benjamin Franklin.* New York: Four Winds Press, 1973, p. 22.

Page 37, line 11: Ibid., p. 25.

Chapter 5

Page 45, line 9: Ibid., p. 31.

Page 47, sidebar: Ibid., p. 39.

Page 49, line 11: *The Autobiography of Benjamin Franklin,* p. 107.

Page 52, sidebar: *Benjamin Franklin* (Fleming), p. 41.

Page 53, line 22: Edmund S. Morgan. *Benjamin Franklin.* New Haven, Conn.: Yale University Press, 2002, p. 29.

Chapter 6

Page 55, line 12: Irmengarde Eberle. *Benjamin Franklin, Man of Science.* New York: Franklin Watts, 1961, p. 94.

Page 56, line 24: *Benjamin Franklin* (Fleming), p. 41.

Page 57, line 3: *The Autobiography of Benjamin Franklin,* p. 185.

Page 58, line 14: Ibid., p. 184.

Page 62, line 24: Esmond Wright. *Franklin of Philadelphia.* Cambridge, Mass.: Belknap Press, 1986, p. 323.

Chapter 7

Page 66, line 11: *Benjamin Franklin* (Fleming), p. 75.

Page 69, line 1: Ibid., p. 84.

Page 70, sidebar: Ibid., p. 111.

Chapter 8

Page 74, line 1: *Benjamin Franklin* (Morgan), p. 220.

Page 74, line 15: Ibid., p. 228.

Page 76, line 9: Ibid., 231.

Page 76, line 23: *Benjamin Franklin* (Fleming), p. 129.

Page 77, line 1: Ibid., p. 129.

Page 78, line 14: *Benjamin Franklin* (Morgan), p. 222.

Page 80, line 21: *Franklin of Philadelphia*, p. 306.

Page 82, line 9: *The Autobiography of Benjamin Franklin*, p. 297.

Page 83, line 22: Eulalie Osgood Grover. *Benjamin Franklin: The Story of Poor Richard*. New York: Dodd, Mead, 1953, pp. 255–256.

Page 84, line 22: *Franklin of Philadelphia*, p. 312.

Page 84, line 21: *Benjamin Franklin* (Fleming), p. 152.

Chapter 9

Page 87, line 1: *The Autobiography of Benjamin Franklin*, p. 300.

Page 91, line 3: *Franklin of Philadelphia*, p. 343.

Page 92, line 3: Ibid., p. 346.

Page 93, line 1: Ibid.

Page 94, line 11: *Benjamin Franklin* (Fleming), p. 159.

Page 95, line 4: Ibid., p. 159.

Brands, H.W. *The First American: The Life and Times of Benjamin Franklin.* New York: Doubleday, 2000.

Cohen, I. Bernard. *Benjamin Franklin's Science.* Cambridge, Mass.: Harvard University Press, 1990.

Eberle, Irmengarde. *Benjamin Franklin, Man of Science.* New York: Franklin Watts, 1961.

Fleming, Thomas. *Benjamin Franklin.* New York: Four Winds Press, 1973.

Franklin, Benjamin. *The Autobiography of Benjamin Franklin.* New York: Random House, 1944.

Grover, Eulalie Osgood. *Benjamin Franklin: The Story of Poor Richard.* New York: Dodd, Mead, 1953.

Isaacson, Walter. *Benjamin Franklin: An American Life.* New York: Simon and Schuster, 2003.

Morgan, Edmund S. *Benjamin Franklin.* New Haven, Conn.: Yale University Press, 2002.

Wright, Esmond. *Franklin of Philadelphia.* Cambridge, Mass.: Belknap Press, 1986.

Brenda Haugen is the author and editor of many books, most of them for children. A graduate of the University of North Dakota in Grand Forks, Brenda lives in North Dakota with her family.

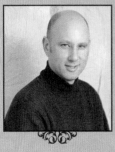

Andrew Santella is the author of a number of books for young readers. He also writes for magazines and newspapers, including *GQ* and the *New York Times Book Review*. He lives outside Chicago with his wife and son.